T H I S   J O U R N A L

B E L O N G S   T O

kickstart

your journal with our free
STARTER PACK

Email us at
gentlerootco@gmail.com

Title your email with our secret code
J877 and let us know that you have
purchased our journal.

Find us on Instagram
@gentlerootco

We create our journals with love and great care.

Yet mistakes can always happen. For any issues with your journal, such as faulty binding, printing errors, or something else, please do not hesitate to contact us by sending us a DM/Inbox at Instagram @gentlerootco

We will make sure you get a replacement copy immediately.

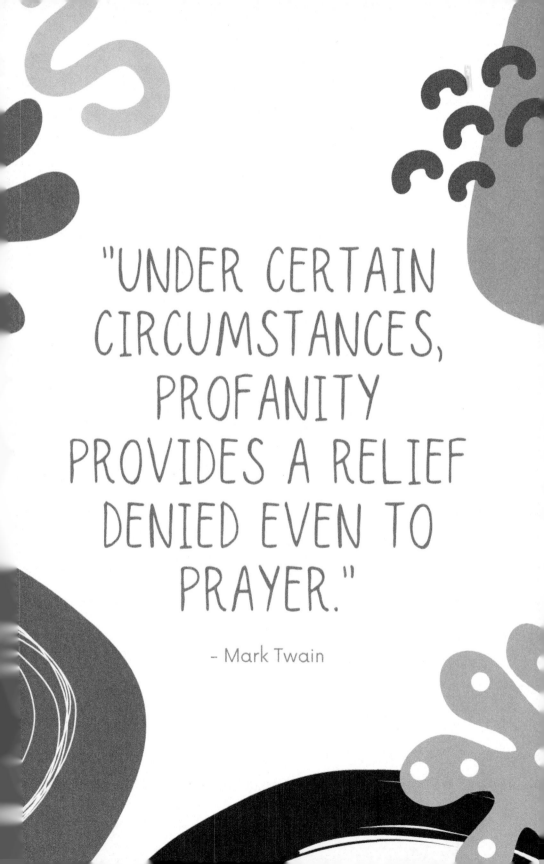

DATE ___ / ___ / 20 ___

I AM GRATEFUL FOR

1. _____

2. _____

3. _____

*
ASSHOLE OF THE DAY

*
TODAY, I AM PROUD I DIDN'T

*
HIGHLIGHT OF THE DAY

START WHERE YOU ARE

Write down 3 things that you would like to receive from this journal. (For example, healthier relationship, peace, reducing stress or anxiety, grief, being in the present.)

1.

2.

3.

Why do you want them?

1.

2.

3.

What are the things you will do to achieve your goals? (For example, practicing 10 minutes a day, be committed.)

_____

_____

_____

Write down 2 things or person that can support you on your journey.

1.

2.

DATE ___ / ___ / 20 ___

I AM GRATEFUL FOR

1. _____

2. _____

3. _____

WTF MOMENT OF THE DAY

_____

_____

_____

_____

_____

_____

3 WORDS TO DESCRIBE MYSELF – I AM FUCKING

_____   _____   _____

WHAT CAN YOU DO TO TREAT
YOURSELF BETTER TODAY

_____

_____

_____

_____

_____

_____

"No one is going to stand up at your funeral and say "she had a small waist and a great thigh gap"

Write down 5 things you **love** about your body and why you are **grateful** for them.

DATE ___ / ___ / 20 ___

I AM GRATEFUL FOR

1. _____

2. _____

3. _____

ASSHOLE OF THE DAY

✳

HIGHLIGHT
OF THE DAY

✳

TODAY, I AM
PROUD I DIDN'T

LIST OF THINGS YOU DON'T GIVE A SHIT ABOUT.

GUESS WHAT! I DON'T GIVE A SHIT.

DATE ___ / ___ / 20 ___

[I AM *GRATEFUL* FOR]

_____

[*ASSHOLE* OF THE DAY]

_____

[TASK YOU NEED TO DO BEFORE
YOU CAN WATCH • *NETFLIX* •]

_____

[WHAT CAN YOU DO TO
UNFUCK YOUR BRAIN TODAY ?]

Letting go

Write down all the **fuckery** and **bullshit** that you need to let go in your life.

Why are they so hard for you to let them go?

"One of the hardest lessons in life is letting go. Whether it's guilt, anger, love, loss, or betrayal. Change is never easy. We fight to hold on and we fight to let go."

- Mareez Reyes

DATE ___ / ___ / 20 ___

I AM GRATEFUL FOR

1. _____

2. _____

3. _____

* ASSHOLE OF THE DAY

* TODAY, I AM PROUD I DIDN'T

* HIGHLIGHT OF THE DAY

Anxiety check in

From a **scale of 1-5**...
What is your anxiety level today?

Write 2 things you can do to reduce anxiety.

I know I am extremely busy and important,
but I promise to do ...

- *IVAN NURU*

"IF IT'S OUT
OF YOUR HANDS,
IT DESERVES FREEDOM
FROM YOUR MIND TOO "

DATE ___ / ___ / 20 ___

I AM GRATEFUL FOR

1. _____
2. _____
3. _____

WTF MOMENT OF THE DAY

_____
_____
_____
_____
_____
_____
_____

3 WORDS TO DESCRIBE MYSELF – I AM FUCKING

_____   _____   _____

WHAT CAN YOU DO TO TREAT
YOURSELF BETTER TODAY

_____
_____
_____
_____
_____
_____

Rage page

There are moments when thinking happy thoughts just isn't going to cut it. You can't be Zen all the time!

DATE ___ / ___ / 20 ___

I AM GRATEFUL FOR

1. _____

2. _____

3. _____

ASSHOLE OF THE DAY

✳

HIGHLIGHT
OF THE DAY

✳

TODAY, I AM
PROUD I DIDN'T

"Talk to yourself like someone you love."

- Brene Brown

DATE __ / __ / 20 __

[I AM *GRATEFUL* FOR]

_____

[*ASSHOLE* OF THE DAY]

_____

[TASK YOU NEED TO DO BEFORE
YOU CAN WATCH • *NETFLIX* •]

_____

[WHAT CAN YOU DO TO
UNFUCK YOUR BRAIN TODAY ?]

I MAY LOOK CALM, BUT IN MY HEAD, I HAVE PUNCHED YOU IN THE FACE 5 TIMES.

PEOPLE YOU WANT TO PUNCH IN THE FACE

Dear

Future self,

I am safe in this body. The
one with the tattered scars
from all the fearless falls.

I love this body. The one with the
stretch marks that contour my hips.

I feel joy in this body. The one with
wrinkles and crinkles, furrows, and folds.

I am strong in this body. The one with the stable
limbs who've carried me through.

I am grateful in this body. The one with lessons
learned and storms endured.

I am this body.

Dear future me,

Write a letter to your future self

DATE ___ / ___ / 20 ___

I AM GRATEFUL FOR

1. _____

2. _____

3. _____

*
ASSHOLE OF THE DAY

*
TODAY, I AM PROUD I DIDN'T

*
HIGHLIGHT OF THE DAY

Self-compassion

How can you be kinder to yourself today?

Self-Kindness -express love and acceptance towards yourself.

Mindfulness – Become aware of what's going on now without judgement.

Connectedness – extend your awareness & acknowledge that everyone goes through tough times.

DATE __ / __ / 20 __

I AM GRATEFUL FOR

1. _____
2. _____
3. _____

WTF MOMENT OF THE DAY

_____
_____
_____
_____
_____
_____
_____

3 WORDS TO DESCRIBE MYSELF – I AM FUCKING

_____   _____   _____

WHAT CAN YOU DO TO TREAT
YOURSELF BETTER TODAY

_____
_____
_____
_____
_____
_____

Define your life!

❖ What are the 2 core values and beliefs that are most important to you?

1.

2.

❖ How does each of them affect your daily life?

❖ What are the actions that upholds and go against your values and beliefs?

__Additional writing spaces available at the end of this journal__

DATE __ / __ / 20 __

I AM GRATEFUL FOR

1. _____
2. _____
3. _____

ASSHOLE OF THE DAY

✳ HIGHLIGHT OF THE DAY

✳ TODAY, I AM PROUD I DIDN'T

Judgement free zone

What would you do differently if you know nobody would judge you?

Listen to your heart and discover your greatest values when there is no fear.

DATE __ / __ / 20 __

[I AM *GRATEFUL* FOR]

_____

[*ASSHOLE* OF THE DAY]

_____

[TASK YOU NEED TO DO BEFORE
YOU CAN WATCH • *NETFLIX* •]

_____

[WHAT CAN YOU DO TO
UNFUCK YOUR BRAIN TODAY ?]

LIST OUT ALL THE THINGS THAT MAKE YOU FEEL

UN
W
O
R
T
H
Y

Pay attention to when these feelings emerge.

Write them down one by one with a different bright-colored pen. Ask yourself why you feel that way and acknowledge them.

Then, reframe them with stories that make you feel worthy. Be gentle with yourself and practice letting them go.

I AM NO LONGER AVAILABLE FOR

THINGS THAT MAKE ME FEEL UNWORTHY

DATE __ / __ / 20 __

I AM GRATEFUL FOR

1. _____
2. _____
3. _____

✳ ASSHOLE OF THE DAY

✳ TODAY, I AM PROUD I DIDN'T

✳ HIGHLIGHT OF THE DAY

LIST OF PEOPLE WHO HAVE WASTED MY TIME

FUCK OFF. THEN KEEP. FUCKING OFF.

DATE ___ / ___ / 20 ___

I AM GRATEFUL FOR

1. _____
2. _____
3. _____

WTF MOMENT OF THE DAY

_____
_____
_____
_____
_____
_____
_____

3 WORDS TO DESCRIBE MYSELF – I AM FUCKING

_____   _____   _____

WHAT CAN YOU DO TO TREAT
YOURSELF BETTER TODAY

_____
_____
_____
_____
_____
_____

WHAT'S YOUR
self-love
L.A.N.G.U.A.G.E

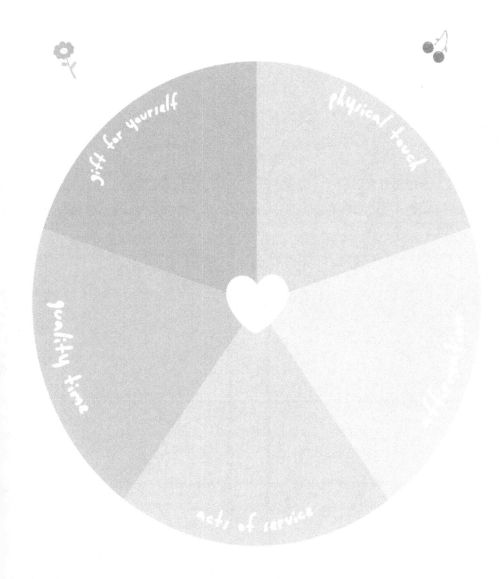

DATE ___ / ___ / 20 ___

I AM GRATEFUL FOR

1. _____

2. _____

3. _____

ASSHOLE OF THE DAY

✳

HIGHLIGHT
OF THE DAY

✳

TODAY, I AM
PROUD I DIDN'T

Color Therapy

COLOR IT'S CHEAPER THAN THERAPY

DATE __ / __ / 20 __

[I AM *GRATEFUL* FOR]

_____

[*ASSHOLE* OF THE DAY]

_____

[TASK YOU NEED TO DO BEFORE
YOU CAN WATCH • *NETFLIX* •]

_____

[WHAT CAN YOU DO TO
UNFUCK YOUR BRAIN TODAY ?]

ANDREA DYKSTRA

In order to love who
you are. you cannot
hate the experiences
that shaped you

DATE ___ / ___ / 20 ___

I AM GRATEFUL FOR

1. _____

2. _____

3. _____

✳ **ASSHOLE OF THE DAY**

✳ **TODAY, I AM PROUD I DIDN'T**

✳ **HIGHLIGHT OF THE DAY**

In The Moment

When was the last time you were so engrossed with what you were doing that you lost track of time?

Describe the experience and emotions you felt. How can you bring more of this state of mind into your life?

DATE __ / __ / 20 __

I AM GRATEFUL FOR

1. _____

2. _____

3. _____

WTF MOMENT OF THE DAY

_____

_____

_____

_____

_____

_____

_____

3 WORDS TO DESCRIBE MYSELF – I AM FUCKING

_____ _____ _____

WHAT CAN YOU DO TO TREAT
YOURSELF BETTER TODAY

_____

_____

_____

_____

_____

_____

Be here now

Get comfortable & close your eyes.

Start by taking a few deep breath

Bring your awareness to your feet and spend some time noticing the sensations, notice any area of tension or discomfort.

Imagine the tension or discomfort decreasing with each breath

Move on to the next part of your body and continue until you reached your head

If your thoughts wander, notice it without judgement and gentle bring your awareness back.

Let your awareness travel across your whole body until you feel relax.

DATE __ / __ / 20 __

I AM GRATEFUL FOR

1. _____

2. _____

3. _____

ASSHOLE OF THE DAY

✳

HIGHLIGHT
OF THE DAY

✳

TODAY, I AM
PROUD I DIDN'T

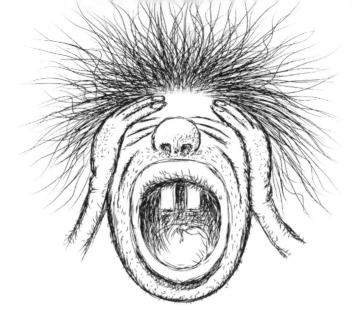

"I HEAR VOICES IN MY HEAD, THEY TALK TO ME, THEY UNDERSTAND"

WHAT ARE THE THINGS THAT YOU WERE TOLD BY THE VOICES IN YOUR HEAD?

DATE___/___/20___
[I AM *GRATEFUL* FOR]

_____

[*ASSHOLE* OF THE DAY]

_____

[TASK YOU NEED TO DO BEFORE
YOU CAN WATCH • *NETFLIX* •]

_____

[WHAT CAN YOU DO TO
UNFUCK YOUR BRAIN TODAY ?]

WHAT ARE THE TIMES THAT YOU WERE RIGHT, AND NOBODY LISTENED?

People might not always listen to you, but the paper always listen!

Write them down.

DATE ___ / ___ / 20 ___

I AM GRATEFUL FOR

1. _____

2. _____

3. _____

✳ ASSHOLE OF THE DAY

✳ TODAY, I AM PROUD I DIDN'T

✳ HIGHLIGHT OF THE DAY

"HAPPINESS IS YOUR
NATURE. IT IS NOT
WRONG TO DESIRE IT.
WHAT IS WRONG IS
SEEKING IT OUTSIDE
WHEN IT IS INSIDE."

- Ramana Maharshi

DATE ___ / ___ / 20 ___

I AM GRATEFUL FOR

1. _____

2. _____

3. _____

WTF MOMENT OF THE DAY

_____

_____

_____

_____

_____

_____

_____

3 WORDS TO DESCRIBE MYSELF – I AM FUCKING

_____   _____   _____

WHAT CAN YOU DO TO TREAT
YOURSELF BETTER TODAY

_____

_____

_____

_____

_____

_____

Love yourself

Write or draw what you love about yourself and decorate them in the heart below...

"LOVE YOURSELF FIRST AND EVERYTHING ELSE FALLS INTO LINE. YOU REALLY HAVE TO LOVE YOURSELF TO GET ANYTHING DONE IN THIS WORLD."

- LUCILLE BALL

DATE ___ / ___ / 20 ___

I AM GRATEFUL FOR

1. _____
2. _____
3. _____

ASSHOLE OF THE DAY

✳

HIGHLIGHT
OF THE DAY

✳

TODAY, I AM
PROUD I DIDN'T

WHAT ARE THE SPELLS YOU WISH YOU COULD PUT ON PEOPLE?

SOMETIMES WE NEED A LITTLE

 *magic*

DATE __ / __ / 20 __

[I AM *GRATEFUL* FOR]

_____

[*ASSHOLE* OF THE DAY]

_____

[TASK YOU NEED TO DO BEFORE
YOU CAN WATCH • *NETFLIX* •]

_____

[WHAT CAN YOU DO TO
UNFUCK YOUR BRAIN TODAY ?]

Write down 3 things that give you the most
E.N.E.R.G.Y

"The things
you do either
give you energy
or drain you"

DATE ___ / ___ / 20 ___

I AM GRATEFUL FOR

1. _____

2. _____

3. _____

* ASSHOLE OF THE DAY

* TODAY, I AM PROUD I DIDN'T

* HIGHLIGHT OF THE DAY

The Funniest

What is the **funniest** thing that has happened in your life?

"LAUGHTER IS LIKE A WINDSHIELD WIPER, IT DOESN'T STOP THE RAIN BUT ALLOW US TO KEEP GOING"

DATE ___ / ___ / 20 ___

I AM GRATEFUL FOR

1. _____
2. _____
3. _____

WTF MOMENT OF THE DAY

_____
_____
_____
_____
_____
_____
_____

3 WORDS TO DESCRIBE MYSELF – I AM FUCKING

_____   _____   _____

WHAT CAN YOU DO TO TREAT
YOURSELF BETTER TODAY

_____
_____
_____
_____
_____
_____

Love Letter

Write yourself a love letter...

Start with a salutation that makes you smile.

Begin with your favorite memory. Point out your charming personalities and lovely quirks, and state why you love them.

Recognize whatever hardships that you are going through and embrace yourself with self-compassion and kindness.

DATE ___ / ___ / 20 ___

I AM GRATEFUL FOR

1. _____

2. _____

3. _____

ASSHOLE OF THE DAY

✳

HIGHLIGHT
OF THE DAY

✳

TODAY, I AM
PROUD I DIDN'T

SHIT YOU WILL DO WHEN YOU ARE **RICH** AS FUCK....

FOR THOSE THAT DARE TO DREAM,
THERE IS A WHOLE WORLD TO WIN.
-Dhirubhai Ambani

DATE __ / __ / 20__
[I AM *GRATEFUL* FOR]

_____

[*ASSHOLE* OF THE DAY]

_____

[TASK YOU NEED TO DO BEFORE
YOU CAN WATCH • *NETFLIX* •]

_____

[WHAT CAN YOU DO TO
UNFUCK YOUR BRAIN TODAY ?]

Superpower

What are your **STRENGTHS & SUPERPOWERS**?

Are you actively making use of them? If not, how can you maximize your strengths?

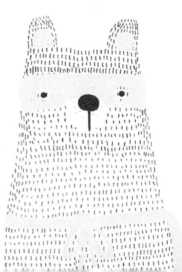

Knowing your superpower
changes everything
-Nadalie Bardo

DATE __ / __ / 20 __

I AM GRATEFUL FOR

1. _____
2. _____
3. _____

*
ASSHOLE OF THE DAY

*
TODAY, I AM PROUD I DIDN'T

*
HIGHLIGHT OF THE DAY

Look back at the photos you have taken 5 years ago, what do you **see, feel, notice**?

What has **changed**?

memories

are special moments that tell our story

DATE __ / __ / 20 __

I AM GRATEFUL FOR

1. _____

2. _____

3. _____

WTF MOMENT OF THE DAY

_____

_____

_____

_____

_____

_____

_____

3 WORDS TO DESCRIBE MYSELF – I AM FUCKING

_____   _____   _____

WHAT CAN YOU DO TO TREAT
YOURSELF BETTER TODAY

_____

_____

_____

_____

_____

_____

WRITE DOWN ALL THE **NEGATIVE** THOUGHTS AND **SELF-TALK** IN YOUR MIND.

THEN, USE MARKERS TO REWRITE THEM WITH A POSITIVE YET TRUTHFUL SPIN ON IT.

Once you replace negative thoughts with positive ones, you 'll start having positive results.

-Willie Nelson

DATE __ / __ / 20__

I AM GRATEFUL FOR

1. _____

2. _____

3. _____

ASSHOLE OF THE DAY

✳

HIGHLIGHT
OF THE DAY

✳

TODAY, I AM
PROUD I DIDN'T

"ACCEPTING YOURSELF ONLY
AS LONG AS YOU LOOK A
CERTAIN WAY ISN'T SELF
LOVE, IT'S SELF DESTRUCTION."

– Laci Green

DATE __ / __ / 20 __

[I AM *GRATEFUL* FOR]

_____

[*ASSHOLE* OF THE DAY]

_____

[TASK YOU NEED TO DO BEFORE
YOU CAN WATCH • *NETFLIX* •]

_____

[WHAT CAN YOU DO TO
UNFUCK YOUR BRAIN TODAY ?]

B.l.u.e.p.r.i.n.t

What losses or "should have been" do you have in your life?

Our Blueprint is the Story We Have in Our Head

When life doesn't go your way, you change your life or change your blueprint. Write down what you will change about your current blueprint.

It's okay not to be okay,
Everyone hurts anyway
Black or White, with plenty or less
We are all trying to hide our mess
Society wants us to always impress
But if your very life doesn't make sense
What good springs forth from pretense

Dearest, it's okay not to be okay
Everyone tends to lose their way
When you feel the lingering weight of the universe
Beating you black and blue, and it still gets worse
Then the times you feel the blade of the knife
Cutting so deep, draining every ounce of life

You watch as your hope crash from the sky
You watch as all your dreams turn bone dry
We all face those times when we ask why

And it's okay not to be okay
Let the pain have its own way
As you retreat to your hideout
And let yourself just cry it out
In your solitude, you will be surprised
By how your spirit will be energized
You will rise above the pain
Break free from that chain
Your struggle won't be in vain
For now, it's okay not to be okay
With time you will fix what's astray

By Irene Agudu Muiri

DATE __ / __ / 20 __

I AM GRATEFUL FOR

1. _____
2. _____
3. _____

* ASSHOLE OF THE DAY

* TODAY, I AM PROUD I DIDN'T

* HIGHLIGHT OF THE DAY

List out all the things that

it's ok to not be ok

Read each of them aloud. Feel whatever emotions that arise as you read. Tell yourself it's okay to not to be okay, accept it with no judgement and be kind to yourself.

it's okay to have a bad day, cry over little things, skip a workout, eat what you want

DATE ___ / ___ / 20 ___

I AM GRATEFUL FOR

1. _____

2. _____

3. _____

WTF MOMENT OF THE DAY

_____

_____

_____

_____

_____

_____

_____

3 WORDS TO DESCRIBE MYSELF – I AM FUCKING

_____   _____   _____

WHAT CAN YOU DO TO TREAT
YOURSELF BETTER TODAY

_____

_____

_____

_____

_____

_____

ECKHART TOLLE

You find peace not by rearranging the circumstances of your life, but by realizing who you are at the deepest level

DATE ___ / ___ / 20 ___

I AM GRATEFUL FOR

1. _____
2. _____
3. _____

ASSHOLE OF THE DAY

✳

HIGHLIGHT
OF THE DAY

✳

TODAY, I AM
PROUD I DIDN'T

Gratitude

Find 2 things that you are grateful for in the worst of times? How do you feel after realizing them?

DATE ___ / ___ / 20 ___

[I AM *GRATEFUL* FOR]

_____

[*ASSHOLE* OF THE DAY]

_____

[TASK YOU NEED TO DO BEFORE
YOU CAN WATCH • *NETFLIX* •]

_____

[WHAT CAN YOU DO TO
UNFUCK YOUR BRAIN TODAY ?]

WHEN WAS THE LAST TIME YOU FELT TRULY

alive

WHAT WERE YOU DOING ?

Chase down the things that
make you feel alive!!!

DATE ___ / ___ / 20 ___

I AM GRATEFUL FOR

1. _____

2. _____

3. _____

* ASSHOLE OF THE DAY

* TODAY, I AM PROUD I DIDN'T

* HIGHLIGHT OF THE DAY

Perfectionism

Think of one perfectionism situation. What perfectionist thinking and behaviors did you engage in? What kind of emotions were present?

Are your standards higher than other people? Do your standards help, or get in the way?

List out the pros and cons if you relaxed your standards.

DATE __ / __ / 20 __

I AM GRATEFUL FOR

1. _____

2. _____

3. _____

WTF MOMENT OF THE DAY

_____

_____

_____

_____

_____

_____

_____

3 WORDS TO DESCRIBE MYSELF – I AM FUCKING

_____   _____   _____

WHAT CAN YOU DO TO TREAT
YOURSELF BETTER TODAY

_____

_____

_____

_____

_____

_____

THINGS YOU SHOULD TELL
YOUR THERAPIST
BUT DON'T...

I was popular once, but my therapist took all my imaginary friends away.

DATE ___ / ___ / 20 ___

I AM GRATEFUL FOR

1. _____

2. _____

3. _____

ASSHOLE OF THE DAY

✳

HIGHLIGHT
OF THE DAY

✳

TODAY, I AM
PROUD I DIDN'T

Forgiveness

Who would you like to forgive? What is stopping you? Have you forgiven others in your life? Have you ever been forgiven?

Forgiveness is about overcoming pain inflicted by another person, letting go of anger, shame, and injustice.

Forgiveness isn't about reconciliation, forgetting, revenge, and condoning.

DATE __ / __ / 20__

[I AM *GRATEFUL* FOR]

_____

[*ASSHOLE* OF THE DAY]

_____

[TASK YOU NEED TO DO BEFORE
YOU CAN WATCH • *NETFLIX* •]

_____

[WHAT CAN YOU DO TO
UNFUCK YOUR BRAIN TODAY ?]

Dreams THAT GOT CRUSHED WHEN YOU HAD KIDS

DATE ___ / ___ / 20 ___

I AM GRATEFUL FOR

1. _____
2. _____
3. _____

* ASSHOLE OF THE DAY

* TODAY, I AM PROUD I DIDN'T

* HIGHLIGHT OF THE DAY

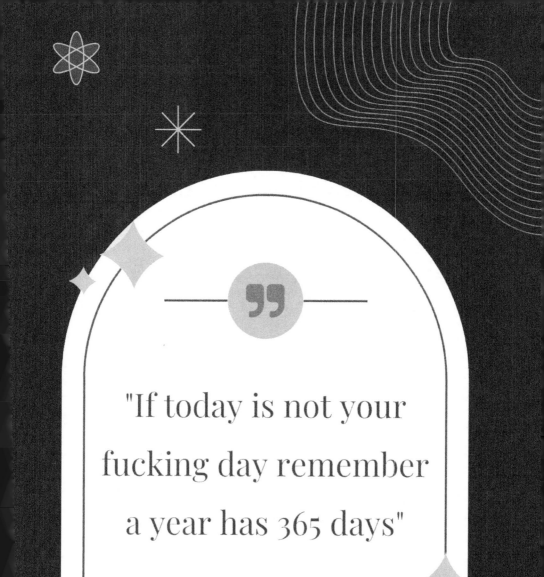

"If today is not your fucking day remember a year has 365 days"

DATE __ / __ / 20 __

I AM GRATEFUL FOR

1. _____

2. _____

3. _____

WTF MOMENT OF THE DAY

_____

_____

_____

_____

_____

_____

_____

3 WORDS TO DESCRIBE MYSELF – I AM FUCKING

_____   _____   _____

WHAT CAN YOU DO TO TREAT
YOURSELF BETTER TODAY

_____

_____

_____

_____

_____

_____

THINGS YOU WOULD LIKE TO TELL YOUR BOSS BUT THAT WOULD GET YOU FIRED.

"

"

"I'D TELL MY BOSS TO GO JUMP IN A LAKE, BUT HE'D PROBABLY JUST DELEGATE THAT TO ME TOO."

DATE ___ / ___ / 20 ___

I AM GRATEFUL FOR

1. _____
2. _____
3. _____

ASSHOLE OF THE DAY

✳

HIGHLIGHT
OF THE DAY

✳

TODAY, I AM
PROUD I DIDN'T

When was the **last time** you did something for the first time?

Was it something outside of your comfort zone? How did you feel after that?

Start *planning* your next adventure.

DATE __ / __ / 20__

[I AM *GRATEFUL* FOR]

_____

[*ASSHOLE* OF THE DAY]

_____

[TASK YOU NEED TO DO BEFORE
YOU CAN WATCH • *NETFLIX* •]

_____

[WHAT CAN YOU DO TO
UNFUCK YOUR BRAIN TODAY ?]

There is nothing like
the occasional
outburst of profanity
to calm jangled
nerves.

Kirby Larson

DATE ___ / ___ / 20 ___

I AM GRATEFUL FOR

1. _____

2. _____

3. _____

* ASSHOLE OF THE DAY

* TODAY, I AM PROUD I DIDN'T

* HIGHLIGHT OF THE DAY

Success page

Write down 3 things that you consider as your biggest achievement in life.

THEY SERVE AS PROOF THAT YOU CAN GET THROUGH
EVEN IN THE DARKEST OF TIMES AND COME OUT ON TOP

DATE ___ / ___ / 20 ___

I AM GRATEFUL FOR

1. _____

2. _____

3. _____

WTF MOMENT OF THE DAY

_____

_____

_____

_____

_____

_____

_____

3 WORDS TO DESCRIBE MYSELF – I AM FUCKING

_____   _____   _____

WHAT CAN YOU DO TO TREAT
YOURSELF BETTER TODAY

_____

_____

_____

_____

_____

_____

BRILLIANT IDEAS I HAD
WHILE POOPING

"IT'S THE UNEXPECTED THAT
CHANGES OUR LIVES FOREVER"
-SHONDA RHIMES

DATE ___ / ___ / 20 ___

I AM GRATEFUL FOR

1. _____

2. _____

3. _____

ASSHOLE OF THE DAY

✳

HIGHLIGHT
OF THE DAY

✳

TODAY, I AM
PROUD I DIDN'T

"TO BE LOST IS AS
LEGITIMATE A PART OF YOUR
PROCESS AS BEING FOUND."

– ALEX EBERT

- NOTES -

- NOTES -

- NOTES -

- NOTES -

- NOTES -

- NOTES -

- NOTES -

- NOTES -

PERFECTLY
IMPERFECT

READY TO TAKE JOURNALING TO NEW LEVELS?
CHECK OUT OUR FAMILY FRIENDLY EDITION

CHECK OUT OUR **INSTAGRAM @GENTLEROOTCO** FOR MORE DETAILS

For any inquiries, please contact us at gentlerootco@gmail.com

Printed in Great Britain
by Amazon

46877802R00066